Biographies of famous people to
support the curriculum.

Mary
Seacole

by Harriet Castor
Illustrations by Lynne Willey

W
FRANKLIN WATTS
NEW YORK•LONDON•SYDNEY

First published in 1999 by
Franklin Watts
96 Leonard Street
London
EC2A 4XD

Franklin Watts Australia
14 Mars Road
Lane Cove
NSW 2066

ISBN: 0 7496 3533 9

A CIP catalogue record for this book is
available from the British Library.

Dewey Decimal Classification Number: 610.7309

10 9 8 7 6 5 4 3 2 1

Series editor: Sarah Ridley

Printed in Great Britain

Mary Seacole

Almost two hundred years ago a little girl called Mary lived in Jamaica, in the West Indies. Her mother ran a boarding house, a homely sort of hotel where people could stay for a long time. Often Mary helped her mother at work.

Mary and her mother lived in Kingston, the biggest town in Jamaica.

Jamaica at that time was ruled by the British, even though Britain was thousands of miles away. Most of the black people on the island were slaves. Even free black people, such as Mary and her mother, weren't allowed to do certain jobs, like being lawyers or doctors.

Despite the rules, Mary's mother *was* a doctor. She hadn't taken any official exams, but she had learnt many skills from older Jamaican doctors. She made her own medicines, too.

Soon Mary decided that she wanted to be a doctor when she grew up. She watched her mother and learnt all she could. She practised on her doll.

Mary had another ambition: to travel. Often she would stare at a map and dream of all the places she wanted to visit.

My father was a Scottish soldier, you know.

When she was a teenager, Mary came to Britain with some relatives. She loved London,

even though children in the
streets made fun of her colour.

Later Mary visited the Bahamas,
Haiti and Cuba, all Caribbean
islands.

In 1836, when she was thirty-one, Mary got married. Her husband was called Edwin Seacole. Edwin was never strong, and when he fell ill Mary nursed him.

Soon Edwin died, and Mary's
mother died too. Mary took
over the boarding house. She
tried to be brave, even when the
house burnt down.

By now Mary had become a good doctor, but she was always keen to learn more. Whenever a surgeon from the army or navy stayed at her house she asked him lots of questions.

So... How is it best to remove a bullet?

She also longed to travel again.
Her brother lived in Panama.
Mary decided to sail to Panama
and see what it was like.

Take good care
of the boarding house,
won't you?

A single woman,
going travelling?
Good Lord!

At that time Panama was a
dangerous place. Many
travellers passed through it.

GULF OF MEXICO

CUBA

JAMAICA

MEXICO

GUATEMALA

HONDURAS

CARIBBEAN SEA

NICARAGUA

COSTA RICA

PANAMA

PACIFIC OCEAN

COLOMBIA

Mary's brother ran a 'hotel' for
travellers that was really just a
dining hall. When Mary
arrived, there wasn't even a

spare bed. The first night she slept under the table with her maid. Her brother and his servant slept on top.

Soon Mary's skills were needed. There was no doctor in the town. When a dangerous disease called cholera broke out, Mary was the only person who knew what it was. Soon everyone was asking for her help and medicines.

The disease spread quickly.
Mary worked day and night.
She fell ill herself but luckily she
soon recovered.

When the town was free from cholera, Mary decided to earn her living by opening her own dining hall. The only place she could find to rent was a tumble-down hut. She decorated it brightly and cooked meals for fifty people at a time. She called it the 'British Hotel'.

The British Hotel did well, but Mary decided to leave and return to Jamaica.

19

Back in Jamaica there was an outbreak of yellow fever. Soon, Mary had filled her boarding house with patients. Mary was also asked to organise the nursing at a military camp nearby.

When the fever died down Mary set off travelling again. For several months she lived in a place called Escribanos, in South America, where there was a gold mine.

Then in 1854, when she was forty-nine years old, Mary visited London again.

That year Britain and France had joined forces with Turkey in a war against Russia. The fighting was happening in an area called the Crimea on the edge of the Black Sea.

Diseases like cholera were a terrible problem in the army camps there. Many more soldiers were dying from disease than in battle.

Florence Nightingale, the famous nurse, had already gone to the Crimea to improve the hospitals which were filthy and badly organised. But many other nurses were needed to help. Mary decided to volunteer.

Day after day, Mary waited for an interview. But no one would see her. At last she was told she wasn't needed. She thought it was probably because she was black.

Perhaps the Crimea Fund will help me.

Mary tried to raise enough money so that she could go to the Crimea on her own. No one would help her.

Still Mary didn't give up. She only had enough money for the boat trip, but she decided to set off anyway. She hoped she would find a way to make her living when she got there.

It was a long journey. At last Mary arrived in a place called Balaclava. Together with a friend, Thomas Day, she decided to open a shop and dining hall for the troops.

At first there was nowhere for Mary to stay. She slept on an army ship, and helped look after the wounded on shore.

Mary and Thomas needed to build their shop. It was hard to find anything to build it with. They even used rubbish floating in the harbour. At last, the shop was ready.

It soon became very popular with soldiers and locals alike. Army food was scarce. Some other shops sold food, but their prices were high. Mary's food was cheap and wholesome.

As well as food, Mary's shop stocked things like boots, caps, socks and saddles. Thieves were always a problem. Once Mary found that forty goats and seven sheep were missing!

You can get everything here, from an anchor down to a needle.

Life at Balaclava was dangerous. Mary's washerwoman lived nearby. One night she and her family were murdered. Mary was often scared, so Thomas lent her a gun.

But I've no idea how to use this.

Although the shop was very busy, Mary believed her main job was to help the sick.

She searched the battlefields for wounded and dying men, even while the guns were still firing. She helped every soldier

Lie down, Mother Seacole, lie down!

she could, no matter whose army he belonged to. Nobody paid her for this work.

Every morning Mary's hut was crowded with soldiers asking for her medicines.

Mary also went out to visit wounded men in their huts, taking them food and drink whether they could pay for it or not. She was so much in demand that she often hardly had time to eat or sleep.

Everyone, from the high-ranking officers to the ordinary soldiers, came to love 'Mother Seacole'.

In 1856 the war ended. Mary was pleased, but she was worried too. She and Thomas had bought many things for their shop that no one needed now. They had to sell them at knock-down prices. Some they could not sell at all.

Mary set sail for Britain. She had no home to return to and no money.

In London Mary found somewhere to live and began to write a book about her life. It was called *Wonderful Adventures of Mrs Seacole* and was published in 1857. It became a bestseller straight away.

By now many of the soldiers Mary had helped in the Crimea had heard how short of money she was. They wanted to help her in return for all her kindness to them.

In July 1857 a festival was held in a music hall in London to raise money for Mary.

There were four performances. Each one was sold out. When Mary arrived the crowd cheered and shouted her name.

But the company which had organised the festival went bankrupt and Mary received very little money.

The Crimean War had weakened Mary's health, but she carried on working. Her friends were still determined to raise money to help her.

At last Mary had enough money to have two homes: in London and Jamaica. She spent the rest of her life in these two places, and she always had lots of visitors. Often they were soldiers whose lives she had saved.

Mother Seacole – do you remember us?

Of course!

Further facts

Jamaica

Jamaica is an island in the Caribbean. People in Europe didn't know it existed until 1494, when Christopher Columbus found it. Then Spain took over Jamaica. In 1655, Jamaica was conquered by Britain. It became an important centre for merchants, slave traders and pirates. Slavery was abolished in 1833, but Britain carried on ruling Jamaica until 1962.

The slave trade

To be a slave meant that you were actually owned by somebody else. You had no rights, you weren't allowed any belongings of your own and you had to spend your whole life serving your master or mistress. For many years British merchants made a lot of money selling slaves. They seized people in West Africa, shipped them to the Caribbean and sold them.

Famous Florence

Florence Nightingale and Mary Seacole both did very important work during the Crimean War and saved many soldiers' lives. But even straight after the war had ended, Florence was far more famous in Britain than Mary. Perhaps this was because Florence was white, and came from a rich English family. Today, many people know the name Florence Nightingale but few have heard of Mary Seacole.

Some important dates in Mary Seacole's lifetime

1805   Mary Jane Grant is born in Kingston, the capital of Jamaica. Her mother is a free black woman and her father is a Scottish army officer.

1836   Mary marries Edwin Horatio Seacole. He soon dies.

1850   There is an outbreak of cholera in Jamaica. Mary learns a great deal about treating the disease.

1853   Mary returns to Jamaica from Panama. There is an outbreak of yellow fever.

1854   Britain and France declare war on Russia. This becomes known as the Crimean War.

1854   Florence Nightingale takes a team of nurses to the Crimea. Mary volunteers, but is turned down.

1855   Mary sails to the Crimea. She helps in the hospital at Balaclava, and opens a shop and dining room.

1856   The war ends. Mary returns to England.

1857   A Grand Military Festival is held in London to raise money for Mary.

1857   Mary's book, *Wonderful Adventures of Mrs Seacole*, is published to great acclaim.

1881   Mary Seacole dies. She is buried in Kensal Rise, in London.